HORN IN F

PLAY ALONG WITH THE CANADIAN BRASS

15 INTERMEDIATE PIECES

CANADIAN BRASS

Trumpets: Ryan Anthony, Joe Burgstaller
Horn: Jeff Nelsen
Trombone: Gene Watts
Tuba: Chuck Daellenbach

T0052882

To access companion recorded performances and
accompaniments* online, visit:
www.halleonard.com/mylibrary

Enter Code
5819-1363-5047-6073

The part remains faintly on the recording for guidance.

Recorded 2001, Toronto; Rob Tremills, engineer

ISBN 978-0-634-04972-9

HAL•LEONARD®
CORPORATION

7777 W. BLUEMOUND RD. P.O. BOX 13819 MILWAUKEE, WI 53213

Visit Hal Leonard Online at
www.halleonard.com

Visit Canadian Brass online at
www.canbrass.com

ANDANTE
from the Trumpet Concerto

Joseph Haydn
(1732-1809)
arranged by Walter Barnes

F HORN

PRAYER
from *Hansel and Gretel*

HORN

Engelbert Humperdinck
(1854-1921)
arranged by Henry Charles Smith

RONDEAU

Jean-Joseph Mouret
(1682-1738)
arranged by Walter Barnes

F HORN

CANON

Johann Pachelbel
(1653-1706)
arranged by Walter Barnes

F HORN

WHERE'ER YOU WALK

from *Semele*

George Frideric Handel
(1685-1759)
arranged by Walter Barnes

PILGRIMS' CHORUS
from *Tannhäuser*

Richard Wagner
(1813-1883)
arranged by Henry Charles Smith

HORN

GRAND MARCH

from *Aïda*

Giuseppi Verdi
(1813-1901)
arranged by Walter Barnes

Grand March from Aida *continued*

THREE ELIZABETHAN MADRIGALS

I. My Bonny Lass, She Smileth

Thomas Morely
(1557-1602)
arranged by Walter Barnes

Three Elizabethan Madrigals *continued*

II. Come Again, Sweet Love

John Dowland
(1562-1626)
arranged by Walter Barnes

Solo; 1st Tpt. doubles on repeat

III. Now Is the Month of Maying

Thomas Morely
(1557-1602)
arranged by Walter Barnes

TRUMPET VOLUNTARY

John Stanley
(1713-1786)
arranged by Walter Barnes

Trumpet Voluntary *continued*

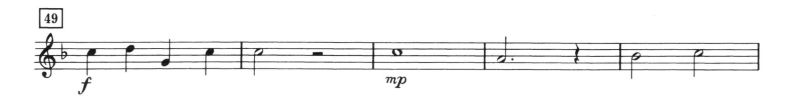

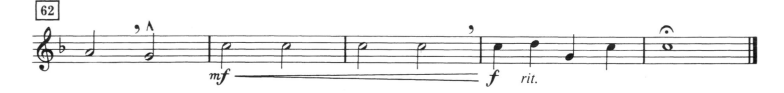

THREE SPIRITUALS

African-American spirituals
arranged by Walter Barnes

Three Spirituals *continued*

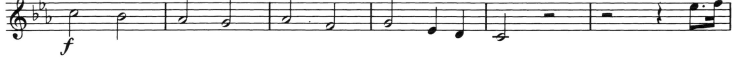

AMADING GRACE

traditional American
arranged by Luther Henderson
adapted by Walter Barnes

F HORN